HOW PUPPIES ARE BORN

*An Illustrated Guide on the Whelping and Care
of Puppies*

HOW PUPPIES ARE BORN

An Illustrated Guide on the Whelping and Care of Puppies

1986—Sixth Printing
HOWELL BOOK HOUSE INC.
230 Park Avenue
New York, N.Y. 10169

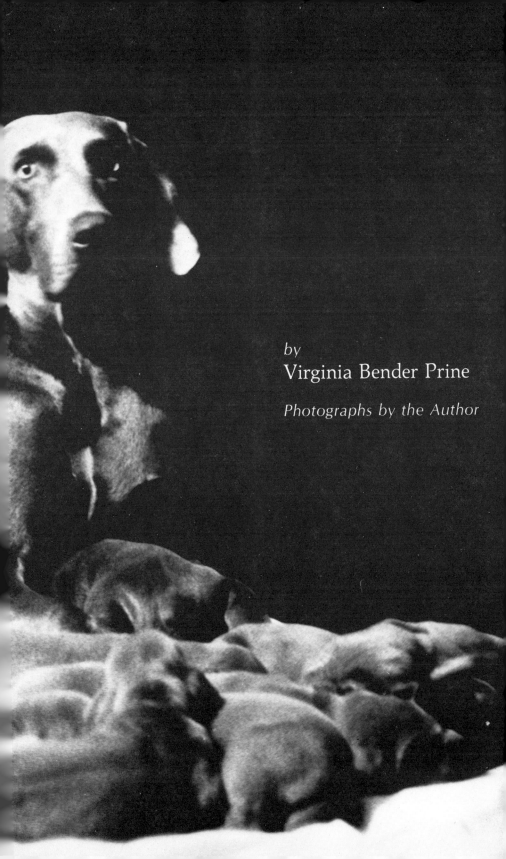

by
Virginia Bender Prine

Photographs by the Author

To
Ginny Lee
who was "almost human"

Contents

Foreword

The birth of young in any species is a great moment for both the expectant mother and, in the case of pets or domestic animals, the owner. In nature and primitive human society, the pregnant female creeps off into seclusion to escape her enemies and to undergo the pain of labor and the supposed embarrassment of parturition.

In modern times, man has successfully domesticated some of the animals in his environment. Science has made a determined effort to study and evaluate all aspects of reproduction, and it no longer remains a dark secret of prohibited discussion. Today, such topics may be studied in a dignified and objective manner.

The objective of this book is to present a guideline to novice breeders and persons interested in learning the basics of canine birth. The emphasis is on the pitfalls involved, and need for reliance upon professional veterinary services for assistance for exigencies beyond the normal turn of events.

As the glory of Spring emerges in all its splendor from beneath the warmth and depth of Mother Earth, so new lives begin. With proper care, nourishment and training this newborn pup develops into man's most faithful and trustworthy companion—the dog.

Dr. C. C. Beck

Director
Animal Health Therapeutics
Parke, Davis & Company
Ann Arbor, Michigan

Preface

IN the wild state, the female dog's entire purpose in life was projected toward producing and protecting healthy, resourceful young who would one day go forth in search of mates and in turn would continue to propagate the canine family. The female dog knew from early puppyhood how to fend for herself in order to fulfill this destiny.

Since dog became domesticated over four thousand years ago, he has come to rely more and more upon man.

Man, in turn, has provided dog with a better and more important place in his own family life.

From early days as a companion to the hunters and shepherds and life under the roughest conditions, to a privileged status as a house companion and playmate, the dog has repeatedly turned to man for his most essential needs.

Dog has become extremely sensitive to man's moods and desires because of the prolonged physical and emotional proximity of the two species. It is, therefore, man's responsibility to try to understand dog's needs and desires and to satisfy them to the best of his ability.

Often, there is complete sympatico between the two. As a result both man and dog are happier because of it.

At no other time is a female dog more dependent on man

than during her pregnancy. It is man's duty to help her during this difficult time.

During whelping, the latent primitive instincts surface and the female dog is generally able to carry on her part of the job without too much outside help. Man's contribution lies in the provision of a warm and comfortable place for the female dog to whelp in a relaxed state and proper attention to her health and nutrition before and after the puppies are born.

The knowledge that man is in attendance and ready to assist if needed will benefit both dog and man. The love and tenderness which new puppies derive from man will enable each puppy to better adjust to his new family when it is time to leave mother and home.

VIRGINIA BENDER PRINE

Acknowledgments

I wish to express my thanks and appreciation to the following Doctors of Veterinary Medicine for their generous assistance and medical advice in compiling this book on the fundamentals of whelping in dogs: C. C. Beck, D.V.M., Director, Animal Health Therapeutics, Parke, Davis & Company, Ann Arbor, Michigan; J. L. Beck, D.V.M; Gretchen Flo, D.V.M., Assistant Professor, Small Animal Surgery and Medicine, College of Veterinary Medicine, Michigan State University; Martin B. Marx, D.V.M., Ph.D., Assistant Professor, Albert B. Chandler Medical Center, College of Medicine, University of Kentucky; W. C. Banks, D.V.M., Professor of Veterinary Radiology, Radiology Section, College of Veterinary Medicine, Texas A&M University; and H. E. Gregory, D.V.M., Confederate Ridge Animal Hospital, Fredericksburg, Va.

Thanks are also due to the following institutions which gave me permission to use their material: The American Kennel Club; The American Field Publishing Company; Ken-L Ration, Division of The Quaker Oats Company; and the Gaines Dog Research Center.

1
Pre-Natal

Assuming pregnancy is definite the birth of the new litter of puppies should occur between sixty-one and sixty-three days after the mating of the sire and dam. Dams that are whelping for the first time may whelp a day or two early.

DIET NEEDS DURING PREGNANCY

During the first half of the gestation period, the bitch will show few symptoms of pregnancy and will generally partake of her usual food consumption and exercise. Additional vitamins and calcium are desirable, though, throughout the pregnancy. These are needed to help the bitch produce strong puppies and to keep her from depleting the calcium in her own body. She will develop a prodigious appetite during the latter part of gestation. Her food ration may be increased, but she should be checked at intervals for signs of overweight. Obesity is a definite detriment in whelping.

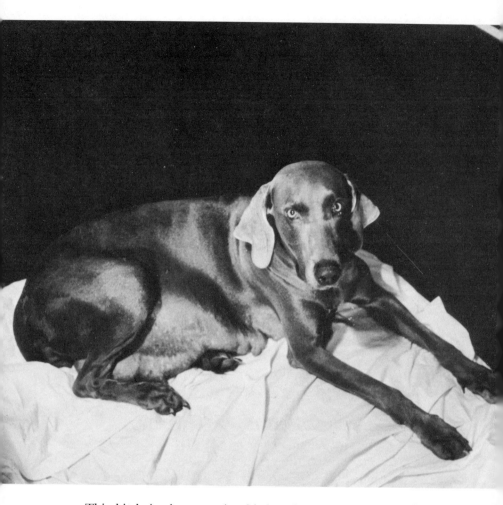

This bitch is about to give birth. Throughout her pregnancy she received the right foods in proper amounts, sensible exercise and required veterinary attention. In familiar surroundings and in peak condition, she will bear her young naturally and with confidence.

WORMING THE BITCH

The bitch should have been examined for worms before mating. But if worming has been neglected, it is advisable to wait until after whelping and the puppies have been weaned, before worming the mother dog. You should be doubly certain, however, to examine the puppies for worms at the first opportunity. An extra ration of food is also advisable, otherwise the mother may lose weight rapidly owing to the double burden of carrying both the worms and her puppies in her body.

PRE-NATAL PRECAUTIONS

An examination by a veterinarian before mating, to ascertain healthiness in the bitch, should be followed by regular check-ups during pregnancy. It is especially important to examine her at least a week prior to whelping to determine whether there may be complications during the birth of the pups.

You should also note whether the bitch's front teeth mesh properly, because, if they do not, she will be unable to sever the umbilical cords when the puppies are born. You must be prepared to assist in cutting the cords, if necessary.

It is desirable to discontinue any violent playing or jumping during the latter part of the bitch's gestation period.

Children should be warned that the bitch's temperament may change as she approaches term. Therefore, care must be exercised in approaching, handling and associating with the bitch just prior to and after whelping.

A few days prior to whelping, the bitch should be bathed thoroughly around the genital area and the breasts with mild disinfectant soap and water. If fleas are present, she should also be thoroughly deflea-ed at that time. Otherwise, the fleas will be immediately transmitted to the puppies causing them great discomfort.

Overleaf: This X-ray print shows the uterus of a pregnant bitch 60 days after conception has occurred. The skulls and spinal columns of the unborn puppies are clearly discernible.

Reprinted by courtesy of College of Veterinary Medicine, Texas A&M University.

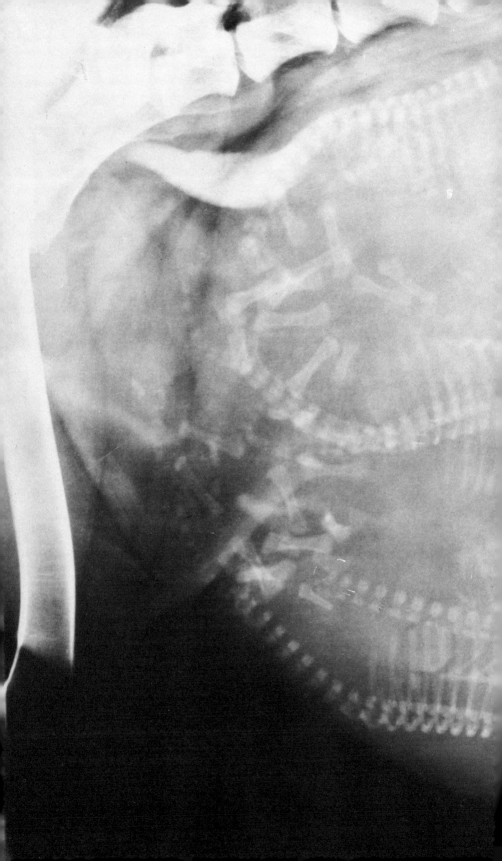

NEST BUILDING

About a week before she is due to whelp, you will notice the bitch digging into the floor, carpets, chairs and sofas or her own bed. This is not meant as destructive action, but is only an effort on her part to make a nest for her coming family. It is another example of instinct at work.

THE WHELPING BOX

At this time you should prepare a whelping box and place it in a warm, dry and draft-free area. If the heating arrangement in the whelping area is inadequate, a small space-heater is advisable. Normal room temperature for new-born puppies should range from between 85 to 90 degrees. This may seem excessive to you or even to the mother dog, but you will find that it is most practical owing to the number of puppies with lowered resistance because of inadequate heat. This is especially true in the short-haired breeds.

The whelping box should be cleaned with a mild disinfectant and placed in an area with subdued light. Expectant mothers naturally seek a darkened area. It may also be located in an area which is convenient to the breeder and where it will be easy to keep clean.

We have found that whelping boxes with flooring built-in are most impractical because they are difficult to keep clean. The whelping box, as illustrated in the section on "Whelping Box, General Information", can be easily moved about for cleaning.

In order to protect the floor under the whelping box and to keep out drafts, place a heavy plastic sheet, several times larger than the box, immediately under the whelping box. A used, clean cloth sheet should then be placed over the plastic sheet and tucked under the corners of the whelping box. The cloth sheets can be changed by lifting each corner of the box for convenient removal of the sheets. The same techniques apply when substituting newspapers for the cloth sheets.

The bitch should be introduced to the whelping box about a week prior to whelping and allowed to sleep in it. You will find that she will appear more relaxed and will whelp in comfort and security if she has had prior access to the box.

2

Labor

The expectant mother's labor usually starts immediately after the membrane sac, in which the puppies are sustained, breaks. This sac contains liquid which appears thick and yellowish in color. The bitch may think that this liquid is from pressure on her bladder and may attempt to leave the whelping box. She should be restrained and forced to remain in the box since labor will start shortly thereafter.

Prior to the beginning of labor, the bitch's body temperature will drop from a normal of 101 degrees to as low as 98 degrees.

Owing to anxiety, the pregnant bitch will begin to pant rapidly. Her eyes will also dilate. Do not be alarmed since this is a completely normal occurrence.

Be alert for danger signals such as:

Throwing back of head and extreme straining during labor
Hemorrhaging
Signs of exhaustion and collapse
Vomiting
Shivering and cold extremities
In labor over six hours without giving birth to a puppy.

The first period of labor is accompanied by a pinkish discharge. Each puppy is born encased in its own membrane sac, and just before the first puppy appears, the discharge will change to a dark red-black color and increase in volume.

The first labor lasts between twenty-five and thirty minutes. Signs of labor are contractions which occur at progressively closer intervals as the labor continues. The bitch intermittently stands up and strains or lies down on her abdomen. The last bearing down in labor comes about with great force and may occur while the bitch is in a standing position.

As the puppy is forced out with a final tremendous strain, the bitch may be in a standing position or lying flat on her side. She will crouch on her haunches and proceed to break the membrane covering the puppy with her teeth. She will consume the membrane as she removes it and will then sever the umbilical cord with her teeth.

The bitch will quite thoroughly cleanse the puppy with her tongue, meanwhile nibbling on the umbilical cord until she has it rather short and neat. She will also lick the puppy vigorously on the face and head to stimulate normal respiration and on the abdomen to stimulate bowel movement thereby assuring proper functioning of these organs.

The expulsion of the puppy from the mother's uterus is followed by further discharge of fluid containing blood and tissue which will turn various colors upon contact with air. The colors range from dark green through brown-black.

Although it is rather difficult to see the position in which the puppy emerges from the mother's body, it has been found that normal delivery may be either head or tail first. Thirty to forty percent of all puppies are born with the tail foremost.

Sometimes two puppies will be born simultaneously—one following immediately after the other. This is because each

The first labor usually lasts between 25 and 30 minutes. During this period the bitch intermittently stands and strains or lies on her abdomen. Strong, high sides on the whelping box are important since the bitch leans heavily on the sides for support.

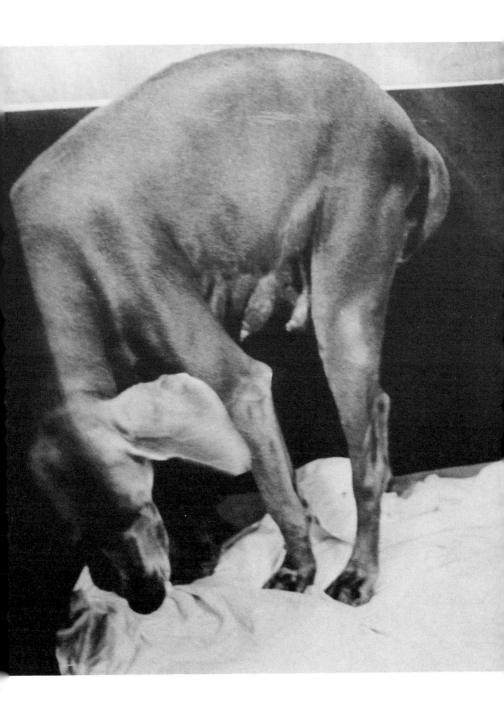

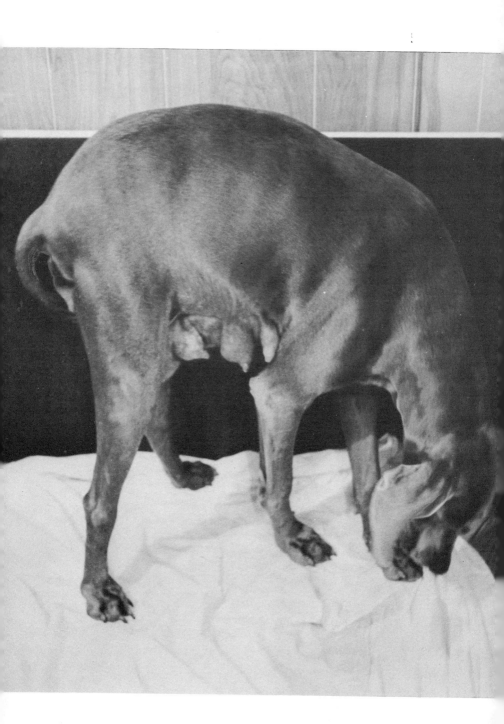

24

puppy will descend from one of the two horns of the uterus. Then the mother has to be alert and do her work quickly.

Although the birth of two puppies simultaneously is rather unusual, the author was fortunate in being able to record this event photographically. See pages 32 & 33.

Under normal conditions, the bitch will clean the first-born puppy and examine it to see that it is breathing and alert. She will then start immediately on the second-born.

However, at this time, the mother dog may need some assistance from you. You can help by cutting the membrane sac of the second puppy with a pair of sterilized scissors. Remove the membrane from the head area only, being careful not to move the puppy from the mother's body.

The mother may now be finished with the first puppy and be ready to take over the job of severing the cord of the second puppy. If not, proceed by removing the membrane from the puppy completely. Cut the umbilical cord about two inches from the puppy's body. A good clean cut is sufficient since the mother will nibble on the cord until she is satisfied that it is the proper length.

You may then proceed to dry the puppy with one of the soft cloths which you should have on hand for this purpose. Place the puppy near the mother's head so that she can finish cleansing it with her tongue.

Puppies generally are active and eager to suckle from the mother within two to five minutes after birth.

If a puppy appears rather lethargic and doesn't make any effort to move to the mother's breasts, you should help it by placing it there. If it still remains disinterested, it is a good idea to remove the puppy to a small box with a heating pad

Labor is accompanied by a vaginal discharge. In the first stages of labor this discharge is light pink. Just before the puppy is born the color of the discharge turns to a reddish-black and increases greatly in volume.

set at about 85 degrees temperature. Keep the small box in the corner of the whelping box so that the mother can see it and so that she will not become unduly anxious about the puppy. In the warmth of the box the puppy will become stimulated and will soon recover from the shock of leaving the mother's uterus.

Within ten to fifteen minutes, the puppy should become active and will be ready to be placed with the other puppies in the whelping box.

There is usually an interval of ten minutes to an hour between the birth of each puppy. During this time, the mother rests or licks her puppies vigorously to clean them and nudges them up to the breast to suckle.

Small amounts of water may be given to the mother between labor. This water should not be very cold. It is wise to give the water in small amounts because large amounts will give the bitch stomach cramps and may cause vomiting.

The ensuing labor pains are generally not as great as the preliminary ones. The bitch should have less discomfort with the birth of the remainder of the puppies. Older bitches that have had previous litters of pups usually have less trouble than young first-litter bitches.

Someone should be in attendance at all times, especially when the bitch is in labor with a new puppy.

The bitch will walk about quite a bit in her efforts to expel the new puppy. In her activity, she may accidentally step on the previously-born ones and injure them if left to her own devices. It is advisable to keep the puppies bunched in an area of the whelping box where she can see them, but where the bitch's activities will not in any way endanger the puppies.

The advantage of the high sides on the whelping box will prove itself when the bitch is in labor. She will get needed support from the sides of the box during labor since she will constantly move about and may lean heavily on the sides of the whelping box.

The whelping will continue for some time, depending upon the number of puppies in the litter. This will depend entirely upon the number of the bitch's ova or eggs which have been successfully fertilized.

All membranes should have been passed within one hour after the birth of the last puppy.

If, at any time during the whelping, a puppy is born without his membrane or placenta, you must be certain that the placenta is passed and not retained in the uterus. In the event that the bitch has not passed a placenta and seems unable to do so, you must have her examined by a veterinarian as soon as possible.

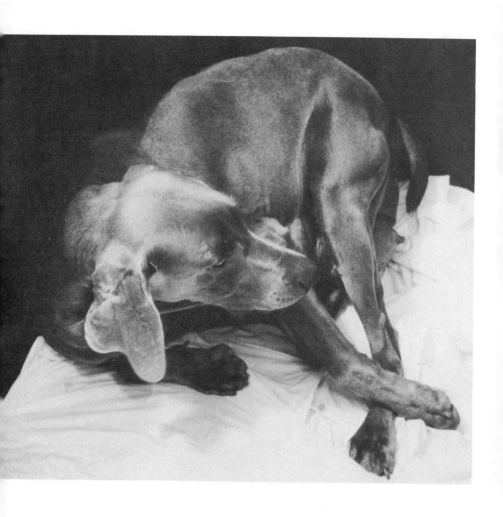

Above: Here the bitch is resting between labor pains. Most bitches will usually lie down on one side as the more severe pains subside. *Right:* The bitch is now experiencing closely-spaced birth contractions. She is bearing down with all her strength in order to expel the puppy.

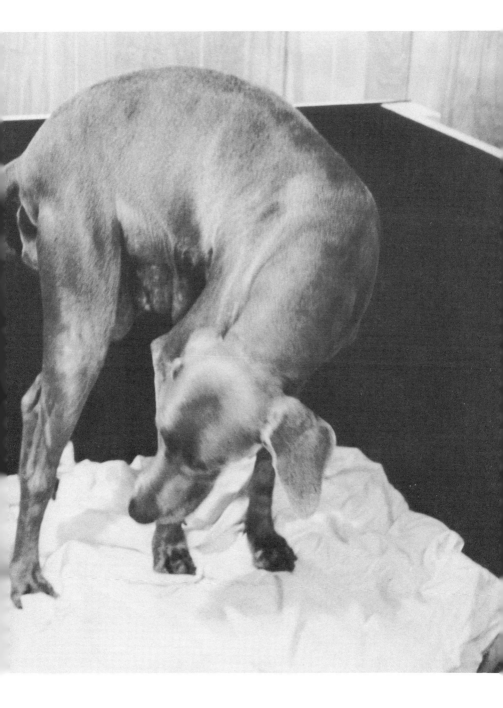

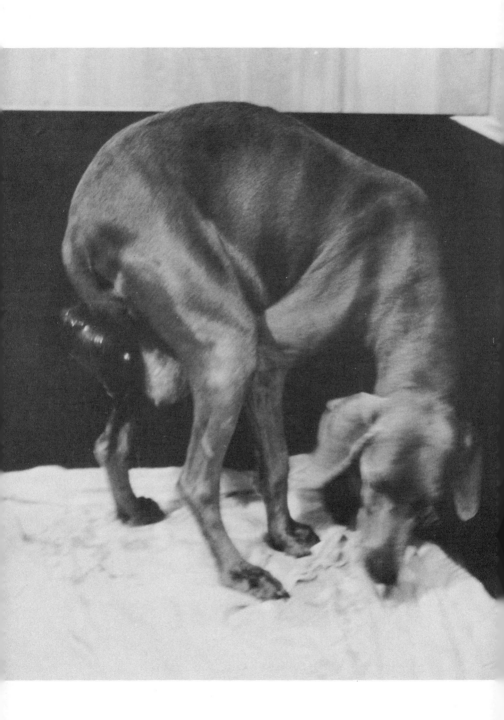

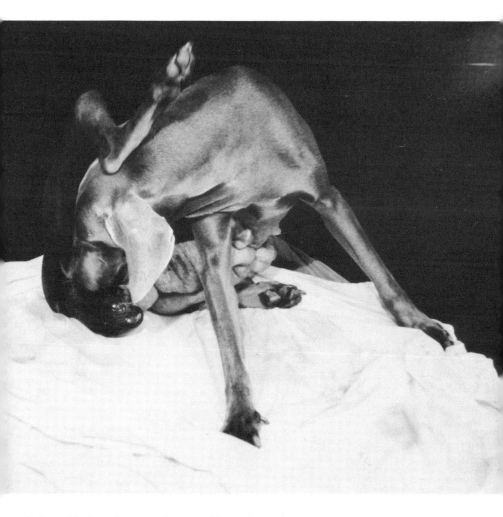

Left: At birth each puppy is normally enclosed in a membranous envelope called the *amniotic sac.* The puppy is attached to the wall of the sac by the umbilical cord. As each puppy is born the mother strips off the sac and severs the cord with her teeth. *Above:* Here the bitch has taken a position that permits her more comfort and ease in seeing to the needs of her newborn. It is at this point that she removes the membrane and severs the cord. If it is a bitch's first litter it is sometimes preferable for the person attending to remove the sac and cut the cord with sterilized scissors.

31

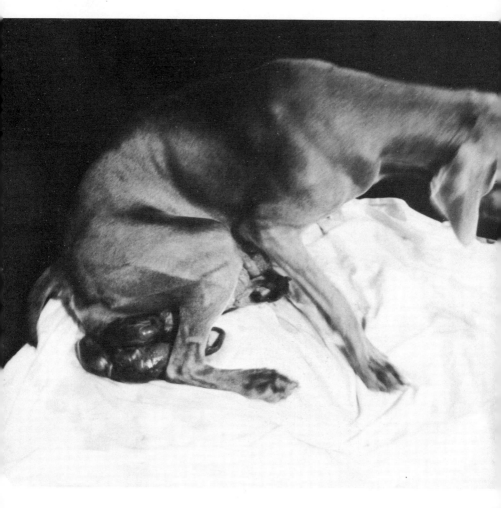

Above: Occasionally two puppies will be born simultaneously as in this particular case. Each puppy descends from one of the two horns of the uterus. The bitch must then work quickly and may need human assistance in order to save the lives of both puppies. *Right:* After both puppies have been delivered the bitch quickly cleanses the first puppy and severs the umbilical cord. She makes certain that the puppy is breathing normally before turning her attention to the second puppy still in its sac.

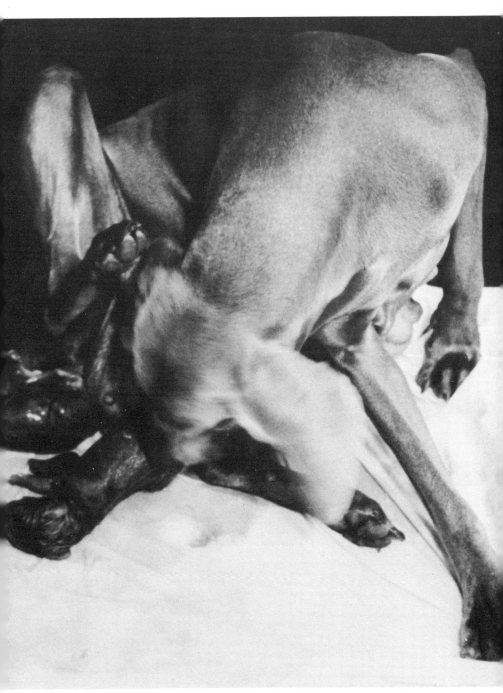

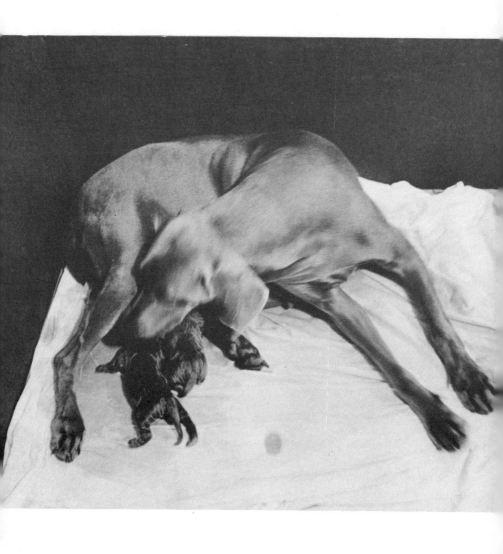

Instinct is very strong in newborn puppies. Although still wet from the fluid in their birth sacs these puppies make straight for their mother's breasts and their first meal.

At this point the mother dog takes a well-earned rest before the next arrival. The puppies that have already been born are almost fully dry and are feasting on the rich, colostrum-filled milk nature has provided for them.

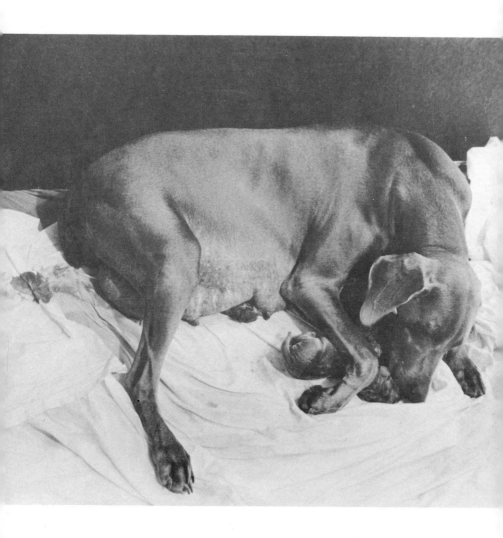

The mother dog will spend a great deal of time licking and cleaning her puppies. This not only serves to remove birth fluids and mucous but also enables the mother to be sure all is well with the puppy and also to stimulate elimination. However, like all youngsters this one doesn't seem too happy about getting a bath!

Healthy puppies will begin to crawl around the nest within a few minutes of being born. Now that the ordeal of birth is passed for these two and they have gained a bit of strength they are contentedly warming, drying and feeding themselves at their mother's side.

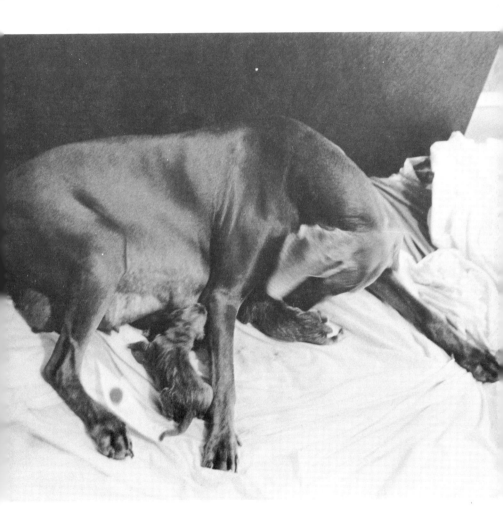

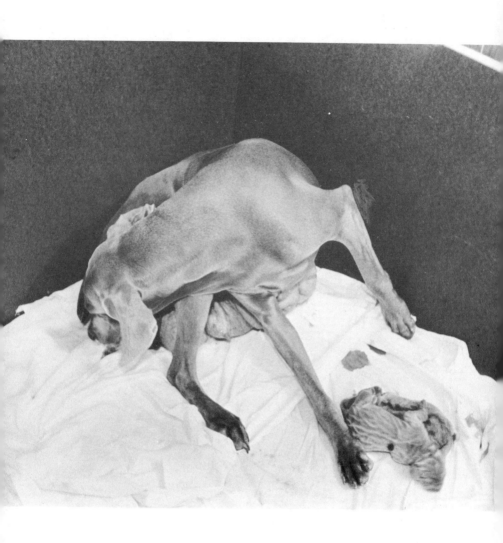

Renewed contractions signal that the birth of another puppy is imminent. With the first arrivals out of her way, the mother dog, acting from instinct, cleans the vaginal area in preparation. This is a holdover from the dog's wild days when birth scents might have attracted predators.

Only the forward half of the puppy has emerged, but the mother is already removing the sac so that the puppy can begin breathing.

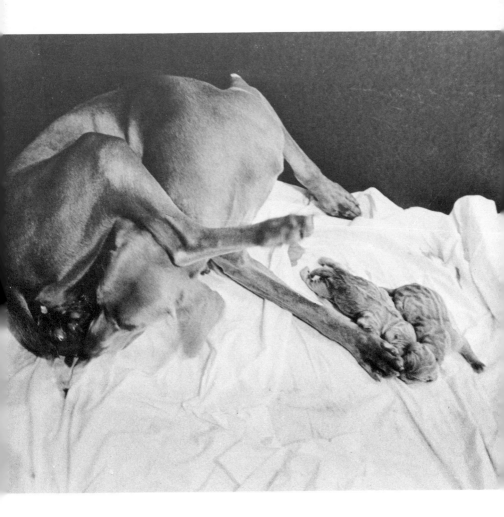

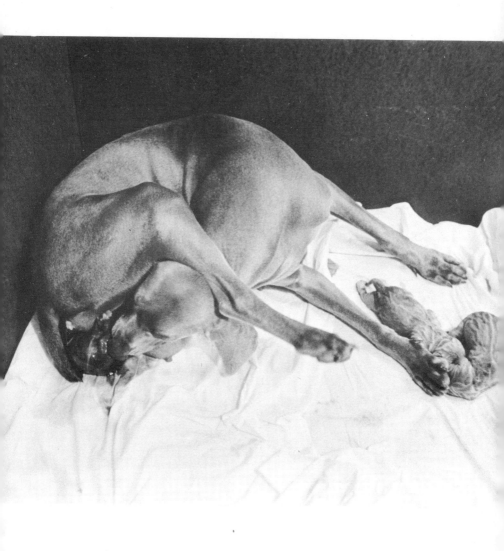

The puppy's forearm has now appeared and the mother bears down harder in order to completely expel the rest of it. The two earlier arrivals, now completely dry and with their first meal inside them are sound asleep and not at all fazed by the new arrival.

Now fully emerged, the puppy is out of the sac. The mother cleans and warms the puppy and will sever the cord as soon as normal breathing begins.

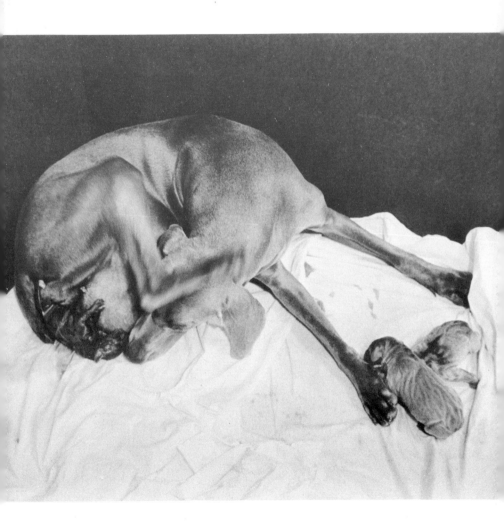

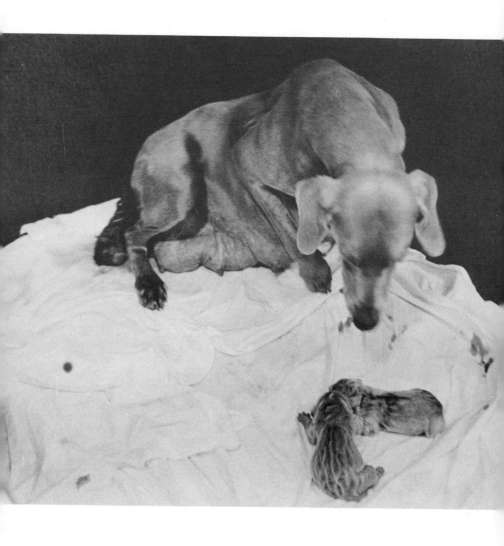

The most recent arrival is very weak after the birth ordeal. The mother dog, therefore, is adjusting her position so she can better administer to this puppy.

The mother has chosen a comfortable position for herself and now proceeds to stimulate the weak puppy. She cleans and licks it briskly to help regular breathing and will encourage it to the breast for nourishment.

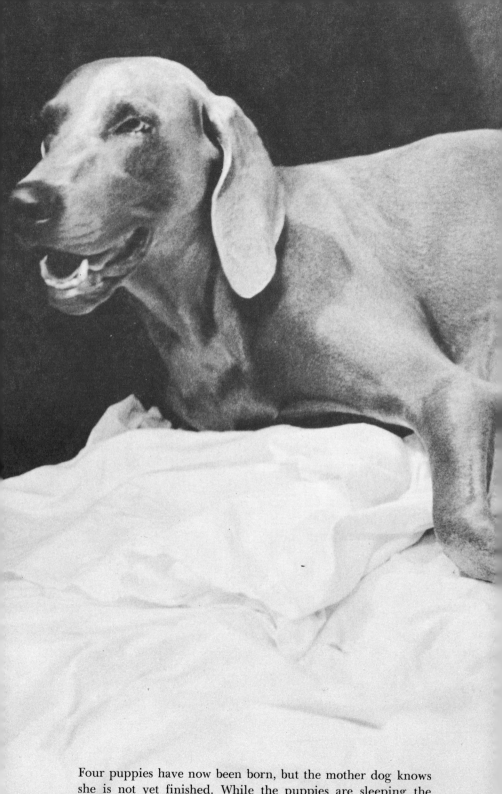

Four puppies have now been born, but the mother dog knows she is not yet finished. While the puppies are sleeping the mother dog also relaxes knowing that all is well and she will soon be finished with whelping the entire litter.

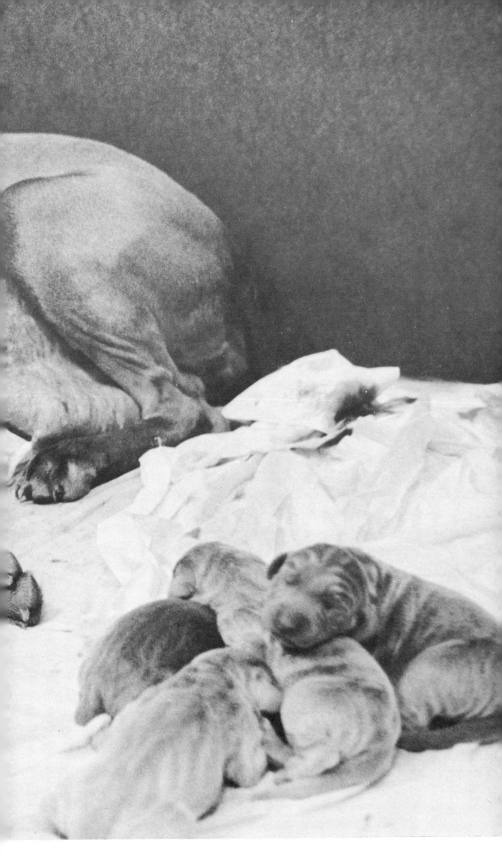

The last puppy is now emerging. All the previously born members of the litter have been bunched well away from the mother, by an attendant, so that they will not be in the way of her cleaning and stimulating their new littermate.

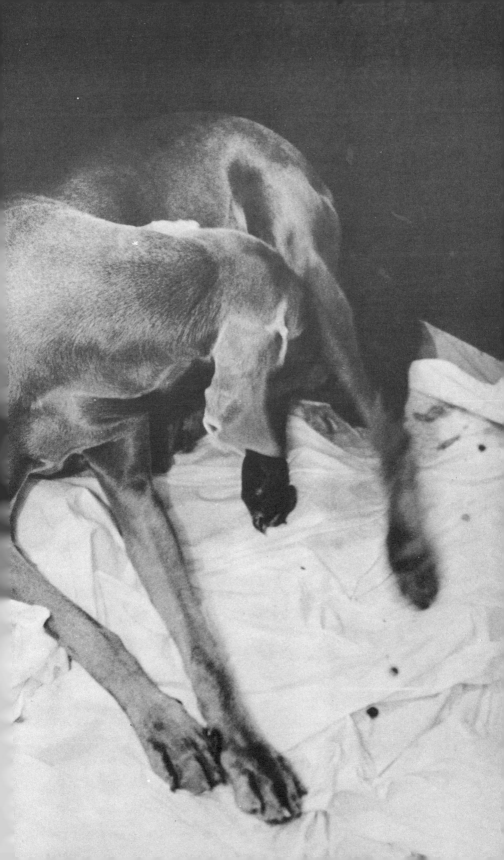

3

Post-Natal

After the bitch has whelped all of her puppies, she should be permitted to rest without any outside disturbances. The puppies should be cleansed by this time and resting or nursing at the mother's breasts.

The mother will continue to clean the puppies and lick their abdomens in an effort to stimulate bowel movement. She knows that the puppies must eliminate the bowel contents after their birth or they will develop abdominal cramps and their appetites will diminish.

Shortly after you are sure whelping is finished, give the bitch a small amount of soft food. Milk may be given *only* if the bitch has been accustomed previously to a daily ration of milk. Otherwise, she may develop diarrhea. The food consumption should be increased for the next few weeks or as long as the bitch is nursing the puppies. Small meals given frequently are better than one or two large ones. New mothers develop prodigious appetites. Fresh water should be available to the bitch at all times.

The bitch will probably need a light laxative on the day following whelping. This is needed to aid in the digestion of the afterbirth which was consumed by her during the birth of the puppies. Several tablets of milk of magnesia should be

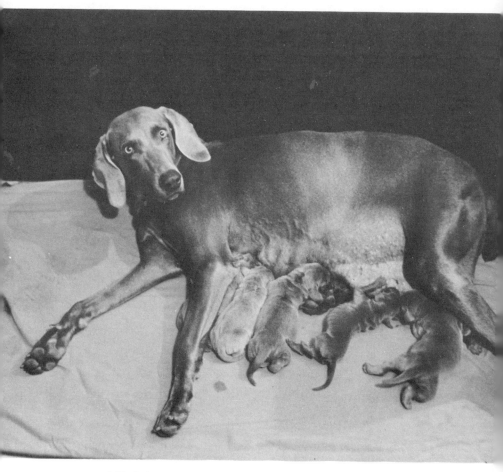

Whelping is completed and all is well with mother and family. The bitch is fully relaxed and is resting while her puppies nurse. The milk of the first 24 hours contains a substance called colostrum which provides the puppies with immunity until they are weaned.

sufficient. This dosage may be repeated within a few days, if necessary.

If it is your veterinarian's practice to examine new mothers after whelping, by all means follow through on this. It may be possible, however, that she is an extremely healthy female and will need only your constant surveillance to check for any problems.

Vaginal discharge should continue for the next week or ten days. It changes from a blackish-red to brownish-red. During the last few days, the discharge should change to a light pink.

In the event of a large amount of bright red discharge over a prolonged period of time or sudden hemorrhaging, contact your veterinarian immediately.

It is highly recommended that the breeder apply a small dab of tincture of iodine to the puppies' navels. This will eliminate any danger of bacteria getting into the body through the navel. The tincture of iodine may be purchased at your local drugstore.

If all of the puppies are healthy and strong, you should have very few problems. But, if one or more puppies are not suckling and seem to be too weak to show any interest, a formula should be made of:

1 cup evaporated milk
1 cup sterilized water
2 tablespoons light corn syrup
1 egg yolk (do not use the egg white)

Use a regular four-ounce baby bottle and enlarge the opening with a large sewing needle. Give the puppy as much of the milk formula as he desires at each feeding. These feedings should occur at four-hour intervals.

The puppy may be held in the normal nursing position or in the position in the photograph on page 53. It may be noted that some puppies prefer the position in the photograph and will not nurse otherwise. However, attention must be given to the amount of milk-flow from the bottle. The puppy's head must be kept elevated or he may gag and milk may get into the lungs, causing foreign body pneumonia.

The puppy may be put back with the mother after each bottle-feeding so that she may lick him and give him comfort.

In the event that the mother completely rejects the puppy after bottle feeding, you must massage his abdomen to stimulate bowel movement. This should be done with a small piece of cotton dipped in baby oil.

The puppy may be kept in a small cardboard box with a heating pad set at about 85 degrees temperature.

The bottle feeding should continue at four-hour intervals. After several days, the puppy may be strong enough to place with the litter and allowed to suckle from the mother.

Even though bottle feeding may be necessary at a later time, it is important for the puppy to receive the first colostrum or milk from the mother's breasts. This milk is high in vitamins and globulin. The globulin is a protein factor which helps give the puppies immunity to the diseases to which the mother is immune.

If it is necessary to bottle feed a puppy from birth, he *must* receive an immunization shot of globulin from the veterinarian in order to maintain immunity in his body.

Sometimes it may be necessary to bottle-feed puppies because the mother has insufficient milk or is ill. This requires only patience, time and endurance on your part.

The author's own experience in bottle-feeding a litter of eleven puppies has shown that a bottle-fed litter has thrived and far surpassed a bitch-fed litter in weight gain. She has also found that since each puppy is getting the same amount of food, the weight gain average is consistent in all of the puppies in the litter. After the first week of bottle-feeding, it was impossible to identify the smallest of the litter.

Naturally, it is easier on everyone if the bitch can nurse her litter. But it should be realized that it *can* be advantageous to bottle-feed your litter of puppies.

Grasping the bottle with its forepaws, this puppy drinks its milk like a human baby. This three-week-old puppy has thrived on a bottle-fed milk formula. After its teeth appear and the mouth changes shape the puppy will be unable to suckle and must be weaned to drink milk from a bowl.

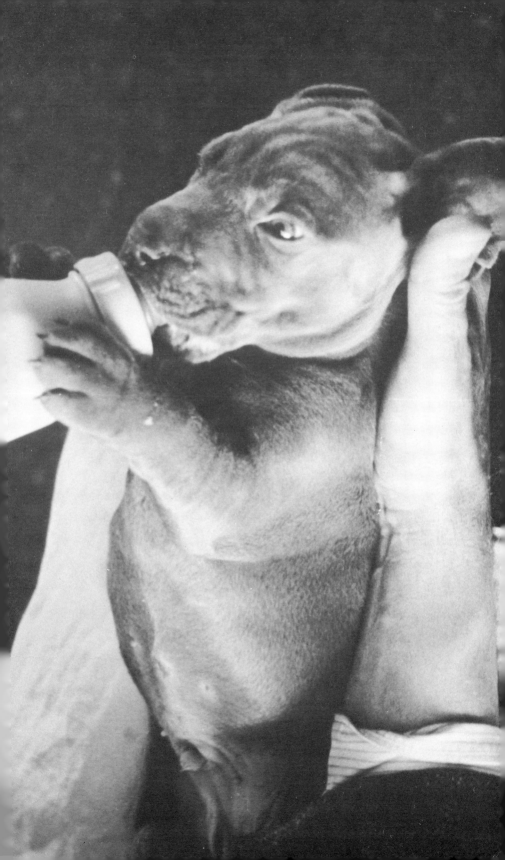

4

Growth and Development

During the first week of your puppies' lives, it is best to keep all noise and activities away from the litter box area.

New puppies, like human babies, need plenty of sleep and food. The mother will leave the litter box only for short intervals to relieve herself and to eat.

The temperature of the puppy room should be kept at 85 to 90 degrees during the first week and gradually lowered to normal of 70 to 75 degrees during the first few weeks. If the room is too cold, the puppies will bunch in one area and may smother. The symptoms of discomfort are whining and struggling to crawl on top of each other.

When they are comfortable and warm enough, puppies will spread out but still try to have physical contact with each other.

After the whelping was finished, the cloth sheets which were recommended for the whelping should have been changed for clean ones. It is advisable to keep these cloth sheets on the bottom of the litter box for at least a week, being careful to change them when soiled. The puppies will have a difficult

This tiny puppy is only two days old. Its rate of growth during the next two weeks is amazing. During this time the puppy's eyes will open, it will try to stand and will even play with its littermates.

time nursing the mother unless they have a surface which they can dig their toes into. After the first week, when the puppies are stronger and more active, newspapers may be substituted for the sheets.

Until the puppies are weaned, the mother dog will instinctively clean the area after the puppies have soiled. But as they grow older, she will become neglectful. This will then become a major part of your chores. The newspapers should be changed as soon as soiled. Otherwise, the puppies may develop skin infections from the bacteria build-up on the floor covering.

Common danger signals in puppies are:

Constant whining	Sudden rise in body
Weakness, depression	temperature
Vomiting	Restlessness after nursing
Diarrhea	Swollen glands in groins
	Small pustules on soft parts
	of body

After the first week, a small amount of handling may be permitted since the puppies are becoming more alert to their surroundings.

Puppies are born with their eyes completely closed. The eyes will open at between ten days and two weeks of age. However, their vision is still blurred and the puppy area should be kept darkened to prevent eyestrain. The color of the eyes usually is an intense blue but may change to either brown or amber depending upon the particular breed of dog.

The puppies' ears begin to open at one to two weeks. As the ear canal opens, the exterior part of the ear will begin to develop. The ears should be cleaned every day because puppies often have an overabundance of wax. If the cleansing is neglected, the ears may become infected. The best cleansing agents are light mineral oil or glycerine.

The nails on the puppies should be clipped or sanded with an emery board at the end of the first week and at regular intervals thereafter. At this time, the nails are hardening and sharp and may cause discomfort to the bitch when the puppies are nursing. This could cause the bitch to stay away from the litter for long periods of time.

By the end of the second week, the puppies will try to stand. This is often very humorous since they are reluctant to give

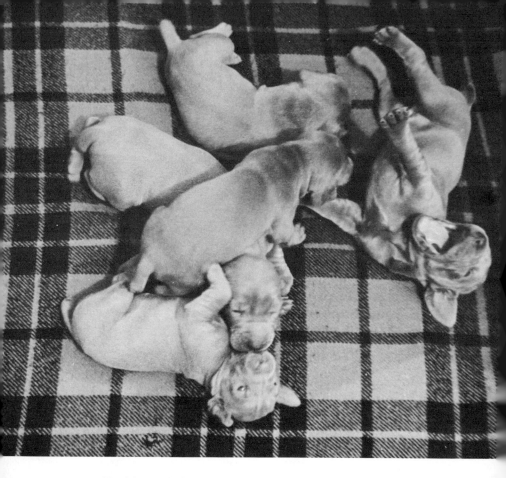

Healthy, well-fed puppies are happy puppies. As their eyes open and their coordination improves, they begin to show interest in their surroundings and each other as the photographer above them is finding out.

up their efforts to stand and will stagger around quite drunkenly. Some breeds are naturally more active at an early age. Therefore, it is very difficult to generalize on puppies' activity growth. The hound and sporting breeds seem to mature physically rather rapidly. Their hunting instincts are obvious at a very early age. Puppies have been known to rub calluses on their thighs while still in the crawling stage because they were very active. This situation can be helped by keeping the puppies on a non-abrasive surface. The calluses may be kept soft with baby oil.

All puppies should have a worming analysis by the veterinarian. Roundworms are common in all dogs and some of the roundworm eggs may have been passed to the puppies via the umbilical cord in the uterus even though the mother has been wormed previously. Worming should be done between the ages of two to four weeks. If worming is neglected and worms are present in the puppy's body, his growth and development may be seriously curtailed.

Some breed standards require tail docking and ear cropping. Check with your veterinarian for the information as to when it is advisable to operate.

While its littermates doze one venturesome puppy tests its sea-legs. Puppies become intrigued with the idea of exploring their home and are very persistent in their early attempts at walking so it is a good idea to provide firm footing for puppies at this age.

When puppies are cold they will pile up to get warm. One danger in this is that the puppy on the bottom might be smothered in its sleep.

Since puppies receive immunity through the mother's milk, they will require immunization shots within a week to ten days after they are weaned from the mother. These *immunization shots are vital* and should not be neglected.

After the first few weeks, puppies require less sleep. They will appear alert and will want to play together. As their eye-

When puppies are warm and content they still seek the physical contact of brothers and sisters while sleeping but not nearly to the extent they do when they are cold.

focusing improves, they will become more and more interested in their surroundings.

Since their previous contacts with man have been pleasant ones, puppies will now begin to show an intense interest in the people around them. This is an excellent time to introduce puppies to children because the puppies are at a very lovable stage in growth. This early stage is unlike the later rowdy stage because the puppy wants to be cuddled and loved. It is an excellent time to establish rapport between the puppy and children.

5

Weaning

Between the ages of three to four weeks of age, you will notice that the puppies are developing their teeth. The appearance of teeth is an indication that soon the mother dog will start rejecting the puppies at meal time. The puppies' teeth are sharp and will hurt the mother's nipples and cause her to stay away from the puppies for long periods of time. It is not a good idea to force the mother dog to allow the puppies to nurse because this will anger her and cause her to reject the pups further.

Other indications that puppies are ready for weaning are crying and restlessness while they are nursing. The mother dog's milk supply is no doubt drying up at this time.

You may now take the opportunity to introduce the puppies to milk in a bowl. The same formula of 1 cup evaporated milk, 1 cup sterilized water, 1 egg yolk, and two tablespoons of light corn syrup used for bottle-feeding is an excellent one on which to start puppies. Do not use the white of the egg.

In order to control the weaning situation, it is preferable to start one puppy at a time. This will not only teach the puppy confidence in eating on his own, but will allow you to check on the slow eaters so that you may be sure that all of the puppies are receiving the proper amount of food.

Hold the puppy on your forearm and grasp his forepaws with your hand. This gives you control at all times. With your other hand, you can introduce him to a small bowl of milk formula. By gently bringing the puppy's nose to the bowl and letting him smell and taste the milk, you will soon have him lapping eagerly from the bowl.

The next step is to allow the puppy to drink from the bowl while standing. Since he associates the bowl with his meal, he will concentrate on the milk and clean the bowl readily.

Within a few days, each puppy should have mastered the task of standing and eating his meal. The entire litter may now be placed around a large pan of food and will be able to eat their meal in an orderly fashion.

At the beginning of weaning, the bitch should be allowed to visit the puppies several times a day after their meals. It will be extremely difficult to wean the puppies if they are permitted to nurse from the mother before their meals. Therefore, if they are allowed to be with her after the meal, they will nurse mainly to satisfy their sucking instincts. This will also give the mother an opportunity to relieve herself of the pressure from the milk in her breasts.

Sometimes the mother will go into the litter box and regurgitate her own meal. It is the natural instinct of dogs to wean their pups in this manner. The best way to handle the situation is to clean it up immediately, being careful not to scold the mother because we do not wish to distress her by curbing her natural instincts.

After the puppies have become accustomed to the milk formula, you may add baby cereal, preferably oatmeal. Rice is good, but also has a constipating effect, so use only when mixed with oatmeal. This should be thickened to make a light gruel.

The first step in weaning is most effective if the puppies are weaned individually. Handled as illustrated, each puppy will soon learn to eat from a bowl. The first meal may be a milk formula mixed with a small amount of baby cereal to form a thin gruel.

Once the puppy associates the bowl with eating it can be allowed to stand on its own during meals. It is better to feed each puppy alone for a bit longer until it approaches mealtime in a business-like manner.

When the puppies have become accustomed to the cereal gruel, you may change to cooked instant oatmeal mixed with the milk formula. The cooked oatmeal has more substance and also is considerably more economical.

If, at any time, the cereals cause a thin stool in the puppies, you may add several spoonsful of applesauce. The applesauce contains pectin and will firm-up the stool.

As the puppies become adjusted to solids, add puppy canned meat to their meal. The texture of the meat should be minced to enable the puppies to chew it.

When the puppies' teeth are strong enough, usually after about six weeks of age, you may stop mixing the oatmeal with the meal and substitute puppy kibble food. You will then have a mixture of milk formula, puppy canned meat and puppy kibble food.

As the milk content in the puppies' food is decreased, it is most important to add both calcium and vitamin supplements. These may be purchased from your veterinarian or local pet shop. Attention must be given to the overall mineral and vitamin needs of the puppy to prevent rickets and other deficiency diseases.

As the liquid content in the puppies' diet is decreased, a plentiful supply of cool water should be made available at all times.

When all the puppies have learned to eat well they can share a common food pan. It is important to watch the puppies during meals to make sure each is getting adequate amounts of food. The food pan should be comfortable for the puppies and large enough for all to use at one time. It should also be heavy enough not to tip over.

6

General Information

American Kennel Club Registration Procedures

It is advisable that the breeder write the American Kennel Club, 51 Madison Avenue, New York, N.Y. 10010, for all forms mentioned herein that are applicable to the registering of a litter of puppies, prior to the mating of the dam and the sire.

The breeder of a litter of puppies is the owner of the dam at the time the dam was bred; except if the dam was leased at the time of breeding, lessee is the breeder.

At the time of mating, the owner of the sire should complete and sign Section A of a Litter *Registration Application.* It should be completed by the owner of the dam or lessee of the dam at the time of whelping, and mailed, together with the fee, immediately to the American Kennel Club. The owner of the litter will then receive a Litter Registration Certificate and a registration application for each individual member of the litter.

No individual puppies from a litter whelped in the United States of America of which both parents are registered with the American Kennel Club shall be eligible for registration unless the litter has been registered by the owner of the dam at the time of whelping; or by lessee of the dam at the time of whelping.

American Kennel Club Requirements for Completing Registration Forms state:

> When the person who owns a litter at birth transfers ownership or possession of one of the unregistered dogs in the litter to some other person, he must complete Section A on one of the individual application forms issued to him by the AKC for the particular litter. These forms are invalid if signed in blank by the litter owner. He must enter the name of the person to whom he directly transfers ownership or possession and the date of transfer in Section A before signing the transfer certification. Even when requested to do so, he must never enter the name of anyone other than the person to whom he directly sells or delivers the dog. He must also enter the color, and markings of the individual dog on the face of the application.
>
> When a dog changes hands more than once before it is individually registered, each person through whose hands the dog passes must sign a separate certification, completing Section A on a gray Supplemental Transfer Statement form (obtainable on request without charge from the AKC) and attaching it to the blue application. These forms, too, are invalid if signed in blank or if Section A is not fully and accurately completed by the signer.
>
> The owner who wishes to register the dog and have the registration certificate issued to him, enters his choices of names on the face of the blue application. If he bought directly from the original owner of the litter, he then completes Section B on the back of the blue form. If he bought from anyone else, he completes Section B on the gray final supplemental form on which Section A has been completed by the person from whom he directly obtained the dog, and submits both of the forms, attached together, to the AKC with the required fee.

(Reprinted by permission of American Kennel Club)

The owner will then receive a Registration Certificate from the American Kennel Club issued in his name for this particular dog. The dog is now registered with a permanent name. The Registration Certificate also lists the breeder's name, breed, date of birth, dam and sire, sex, color and markings. No amount of transfers of ownership will alter this registration.

If American Kennel Club registration papers are not available at the time puppy is shipped or delivered to someone else, person delivering or shipping puppy must furnish with the puppy a bill of sale or other signed memorandum stating all identifying information such as: breed, sex and color and markings, date of birth, litter number (when available), names of sire and dam, name of breeder, and date sold or delivered.

It is good practice to keep accurate records of each litter whelped. These records should include names of sire and dam, date of whelping, number of puppies whelped by sex and by color and markings, litter registration number, date of sale, gift or death of each puppy so described, name and address of person acquiring each puppy, kind of papers and date supplied, registered name and number of each puppy registered by breeder.

The American Kennel Club Dog Record Book is an excellent and easy way to keep your ownership and breeding records. It can be purchased from Record Book Department, The American Kennel Club, Inc., 51 Madison Avenue, New York, N.Y. 10010.

Field Dog Stud Book Registration Procedures

The Field Dog Stud Book functions as a registry for all breeds of dogs, records names, colors, ages, pedigrees, sex, Transfer of Ownership and enrolls litters.

All forms applicable to the registering of a litter of puppies may be obtained from The American Field Publishing Company, 222 West Adams St., Chicago, Illinois 60606.

Litters of puppies are registered by submitting an Application for Enrollment of Litter together with the fee. The application must be accompanied by a pink Certificate for Owner of Bitch and a blue Certificate for Owner of Stud Dog.

Upon the enrollment of a litter, each puppy is registered and numbered separately on the Field Dog Stud Book enrollment record.

Certificates of Enrollment for each individual puppy are then issued to the breeder. A Certificate of Enrollment must accompany each puppy that is sold from a litter so that it may be mailed along with the Field Dog Stud Book Application for Registration for the permanent registration of the puppy.

The litter should be enrolled because it establishes a complete and accurate record of the entire litter.

Enrollment of the litter eliminates the need to submit a blue Certificate for Owner of Stud Dog when application is made for registration of each of the previously enrolled pups in the litter.

The Field Dog Stud Application for Registration is for the purpose of obtaining a Certificate of Registration for each individual puppy.

It includes application for a name and allows three choices, the maximum being three words or twenty letters. Numerals or Jrs. used in consecutive order in the name are counted as words.

Changes of names are permitted for a period of one year only from the date of the original registration.

The Pedigree Form and How to Use It

The Pedigree is simply a family tree. It enables the breeder to determine the names and characteristics of the ancestral male and female dogs in the lineage. It also shows whether the breeders concerned have carried out in-breeding or line-breeding.

In-breeding is the mating of a male and female who are

CERTIFIED PEDIGREE

BREED_____ COLOR AND/OR MARKINGS_____ SEX____ DATE WHELPED_____

CALL NAME_____ BREEDER_____ ADDRESS_____

REG. NAME_____ A.K.C. REG. No._____ SELLER_____

Sire

Sire

Dam

Dam

Sire

Sire

Dam

Dam

Sire

Sire

Dam

Dam

Sire

Sire

Dam

Dam

Sire

Sire

Dam

Dam

Sire

Sire

Dam

Dam

Sire

Sire

Dam

Dam

Sire

Sire

Dam

Dam

I hereby certify that this Pedigree is true to the best of my knowledge _____
Signed

Reprinted by permission of Ken-L Ration, A Division of The Quaker Oats Company.

A typical four-generation pedigree is an invaluable tool for those working out a breeding program. Knowing a dog's ancestors helps to visualize what the dog is able to produce in his offspring.

closely related, such as brother and sister, mother and son or father and daughter.

Line-breeding is the bringing together of two members of the opposite sex who have the same ancestors, for example — grandmother, grandfather, aunt or uncle.

The careful study of your dog's pedigree will enable you to determine the general characteristics of each dog. You will also be able to determine whether any faults have been injected into the line. Careful selection of mates can help you to avoid dogs carrying these undesirable traits.

Sixty-Three Day Whelping Calendar

Find the month and date on which your bitch was bred in one of the left-hand columns. Directly opposite that date, in the right-hand column, is her expected date of whelping, bearing in mind that 61 days is as common as 63.

Date bred (January)	Date due to whelp (March)	Date bred (February)	Date due to whelp (April)	Date bred (March)	Date due to whelp (May)	Date bred (April)	Date due to whelp (June)	Date bred (May)	Date due to whelp (July)	Date bred (June)	Date due to whelp (August)	Date bred (July)	Date due to whelp (September)	Date bred (August)	Date due to whelp (October)	Date bred (September)	Date due to whelp (November)	Date bred (October)	Date due to whelp (December)	Date bred (November)	Date due to whelp (January)	Date bred (December)	Date due to whelp (February)
1	5	1	5	1	3	1	3	1	3	1	3	1	2	1	3	1	3	1	3	1	3	1	2
2	6	2	6	2	4	2	4	2	4	2	4	2	3	2	4	2	4	2	4	2	4	2	3
3	7	3	7	3	5	3	5	3	5	3	5	3	4	3	5	3	5	3	5	3	5	3	4
4	8	4	8	4	6	4	6	4	6	4	6	4	5	4	6	4	6	4	6	4	6	4	5
5	9	5	9	5	7	5	7	5	7	5	7	5	6	5	7	5	7	5	7	5	7	5	6
6	10	6	10	6	8	6	8	6	8	6	8	6	7	6	8	6	8	6	8	6	8	6	7
7	11	7	11	7	9	7	9	7	9	7	9	7	8	7	9	7	9	7	9	7	9	7	8
8	12	8	12	8	10	8	10	8	10	8	10	8	9	8	10	8	10	8	10	8	10	8	9
9	13	9	13	9	11	9	11	9	11	9	11	9	10	9	11	9	11	9	11	9	11	9	10
10	14	10	14	10	12	10	12	10	12	10	12	10	11	10	12	10	12	10	12	10	12	10	11
11	15	11	15	11	13	11	13	11	13	11	13	11	12	11	13	11	13	11	13	11	13	11	12
12	16	12	16	12	14	12	14	12	14	12	14	12	13	12	14	12	14	12	14	12	14	12	13
13	17	13	17	13	15	13	15	13	15	13	15	13	14	13	15	13	15	13	15	13	15	13	14
14	18	14	18	14	16	14	16	14	16	14	16	14	15	14	16	14	16	14	16	14	16	14	15
15	19	15	19	15	17	15	17	15	17	15	17	15	16	15	17	15	17	15	17	15	17	15	16
16	20	16	20	16	18	16	18	16	18	16	18	16	17	16	18	16	18	16	18	16	18	16	17
17	21	17	21	17	19	17	19	17	19	17	19	17	18	17	19	17	19	17	19	17	19	17	18
18	22	18	22	18	20	18	20	18	20	18	20	18	19	18	20	18	20	18	20	18	20	18	19
19	23	19	23	19	21	19	21	19	21	19	21	19	20	19	21	19	21	19	21	19	21	19	20
20	24	20	24	20	22	20	22	20	22	20	22	20	21	20	22	20	22	20	22	20	22	20	21
21	25	21	25	21	23	21	23	21	23	21	23	21	22	21	23	21	23	21	23	21	23	21	22
22	26	22	26	22	24	22	24	22	24	22	24	22	23	22	24	22	24	22	24	22	24	22	23
23	27	23	27	23	25	23	25	23	25	23	25	23	24	23	25	23	25	23	25	23	25	23	24
24	28	24	28	24	26	24	26	24	26	24	26	24	25	24	26	24	26	24	26	24	26	24	25
25	29	25	29	25	27	25	27	25	27	25	27	25	26	25	27	25	27	25	27	25	27	25	26
26	30	26	30	26	28	26	28	26	28	26	28	26	27	26	28	26	28	26	28	26	28	26	27
27	31	27	1 May	27	29	27	29	27	29	27	29	27	28	27	29	27	29	27	29	27	29	27	28
28	1 Apr.	28	2	28	30	28	30	28	30	28	30	28	29	28	30	28	30	28	30	28	30	28	1 Mar.
29	2			29	31	29	1 July	29	31	29	31	29	30	29	31	29	1 Dec.	29	31	29	31	29	2
30	3			30	1 June	30	2	30	1 Aug.	30	1 Sep.	30	1 Oct.	30	1 Nov.	30	2	30	1 Jan.	30	1 Feb.	30	3
31	4			31	2			31	2			31	2	31	2			31	2			31	4

Building a Whelping Box

The Whelping Box is made up of:

one 4 ft. x 8 ft. sheet of masonite board
(cut in 4–2' x 4' pieces)

four 2 in. x 4 in. pieces of board
(cut in 2 ft. lengths)

four 1 in. x 2 in. pieces of board
(cut in 4 ft. lengths)

The masonite board is smooth on one side only. Be sure to use the smooth side inside the box.

The 1 in. x 2 in. boards are nailed or screwed to the outside of the masonite boards with the nail heads inside the box.

After assembling the masonite boards and 1 in. x 2 in. boards, fasten a 2 in. x 4 in. board to each corner of the front of the box (one section of masonite should have a small opening as illustrated in the drawing.)

Proceed to nail or screw the sections together at the corners, continuing around the box. All of your boards must be on the outside of the box, making certain that only the nailheads (nailed well into the boards) are on the inside of the box.

This box may be taken apart at the corners and stored between litters.

Because there is no bottom on the box, place box on a large heavy plastic sheet covered by a cloth sheet. This allows for easy cleaning.

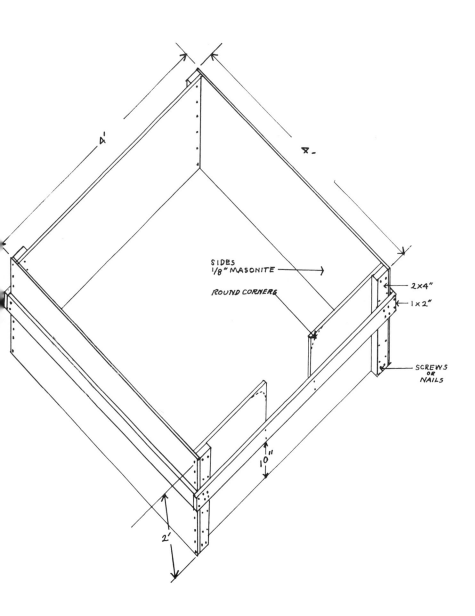

4'

4'

SIDES
1/8" MASONITE

ROUND CORNERS

2×4"

1×2"

SCREWS
OR
NAILS

10"

2'

77

Materials Needed During Whelping

Whelping box
Large, heavy plastic sheet
Several used, clean cloth sheets
Newspapers (clean)
Space heater with thermostat controls or
    Infra-ray bulb for additional heat
Cardboard box (approx. 12″ x 12″)
Heating pad with thermostat controls or
    Hot water bottle
Several soft, flannel cloths (pre-washed)
Scissors (sharp and sterilized)
Baby nursing bottle with small-sized nipple
Evaporated milk
Eggs
Corn syrup, light
Mineral oil or glycerine for ear cleaning
Nail file or emery board for puppies' nails
Rectal thermometer
Milk of magnesia
Tincture of iodine

Glossary

Afterbirth	the placenta and membranes with which the fetus is connected, expelled after delivery
Bitch	a female dog
Breed	to reproduce young
Breeder	one who produces animals and their off-spring
Colostrum	first milk from mother's breasts which is high in vitamins and globulin
Dam	the female parent
Fetus	the young of an animal in the womb

78

Genitals	the external sexual organs
Gestation	period of carrying young in the uterus
Globulin	protein factor which gives puppies immunity to the diseases to which the mother is immune
Litter	the puppies of one whelping
Mate	to breed a dog and a bitch
Membrane sac	thin, soft pliable skin covering the puppy in the uterus
Ova	reproductive eggs produced in the ovaries of the female
Placenta	the vascular structure by which the fetus is nourished in the uterus
Pregnancy	condition of being with young
Sire	the male parent
Umbilical cord	cord arising from the navel of the fetus which connects with the placenta or afterbirth
Uterus	an organ for containing and nourishing young prior to birth
Vagina	a canal which leads from the uterus to the external orifice of the genital canal; specifically in female animals
Wean	to accustom the puppy to loss of the mother's milk
Whelp	to give birth to young

BIBLIOGRAPHY

ALL OWNERS of pure-bred dogs will benefit themselves and their dogs by enriching their knowledge of br
and of canine care, training, breeding, psychology and other important aspects of dog management. The fol
ing list of books covers further reading recommended by judges, veterinarians, breeders, trainers and other author
Books may be obtained at the finer book stores and pet shops, or through Howell Book House Inc., publis
New York.

BREED BOOKS

AFGHAN HOUND, Complete	Miller & Gilbert
AIREDALE, New Complete	Edwards
AKITA, Complete	Linderman & Funk
ALASKAN MALAMUTE, Complete	Riddle & Seeley
BASSET HOUND, Complete	Braun
BLOODHOUND, Complete	Brey & Reed
BOXER, Complete	Denlinger
BRITTANY SPANIEL, Complete	Riddle
BULLDOG, New Complete	Hanes
BULL TERRIER, New Complete	Eberhard
CAIRN TERRIER, Complete	Marvin
CHESAPEAKE BAY RETRIEVER, Complete	Cherry
CHIHUAHUA, Complete	Noted Authorities
COCKER SPANIEL, New	Kraeuchi
COLLIE, New	Official Publication of the Collie Club of America
DACHSHUND, The New	Meistrell
DALMATIAN, The	Treen
DOBERMAN PINSCHER, New	Walker
ENGLISH SETTER, New Complete	Tuck, Howell & Graef
ENGLISH SPRINGER SPANIEL, New	Goodall & Gasow
FOX TERRIER, New	Nedell
GERMAN SHEPHERD DOG, New Complete	Bennett
GERMAN SHORTHAIRED POINTER, New	Maxwell
GOLDEN RETRIEVER, New Complete	Fischer
GORDON SETTER, Complete	Look
GREAT DANE, New Complete	Noted Authorities
GREAT DANE, The—Dogdom's Apollo	Draper
GREAT PYRENEES, Complete	Strang & Giffin
IRISH SETTER, New Complete	Eldredge & Vanacore
IRISH WOLFHOUND, Complete	Starbuck
JACK RUSSELL TERRIER, Complete	Plummer
KEESHOND, New Complete	Cash
LABRADOR RETRIEVER, Complete	Warwick
LHASA APSO, Complete	Herbel
MASTIFF, History and Management of the	Baxter & Hoffman
MINIATURE SCHNAUZER, Complete	Eskrigge
NEWFOUNDLAND, New Complete	Chern
NORWEGIAN ELKHOUND, New Complete	Wallo
OLD ENGLISH SHEEPDOG, Complete	Mandeville
PEKINGESE, Quigley Book of	Quigley
PEMBROKE WELSH CORGI, Complete	Sargent & Harper
POODLE, New	Irick
POODLE CLIPPING AND GROOMING BOOK, Complete	Kalstone
ROTTWEILER, Complete	Freeman
SAMOYED, New Complete	Ward
SCOTTISH TERRIER, New Complete	Marvin
SHETLAND SHEEPDOG, The New	Riddle
SHIH TZU, Joy of Owning	Seranne
SHIH TZU, The (English)	Dadds
SIBERIAN HUSKY, Complete	Demidoff
TERRIERS, The Book of All	Marvin
WEIMARANER, Guide to the	Burgoin
WEST HIGHLAND WHITE TERRIER, Complete	Marvin
WHIPPET, Complete	Pegram
YORKSHIRE TERRIER, Complete	Gordon & Bennett

BREEDING

ART OF BREEDING BETTER DOGS, New	Onstott
BREEDING YOUR OWN SHOW DOG	Seranne
HOW TO BREED DOGS	Whitney
HOW PUPPIES ARE BORN	Prine
INHERITANCE OF COAT COLOR IN DOGS	Little

CARE AND TRAINING

COUNSELING DOG OWNERS, Evans Guide for	E
DOG OBEDIENCE, Complete Book of	Saun
NOVICE, OPEN AND UTILITY COURSES	Saur
DOG CARE AND TRAINING FOR BOYS AND GIRLS	Saur
DOG NUTRITION, Collins Guide to	C
DOG TRAINING FOR KIDS	Benj
DOG TRAINING, Koehler Method of	Ko
DOG TRAINING Made Easy	T
GO FIND! Training Your Dog to Track	L
GUARD DOG TRAINING, Koehler Method of	Ko
MOTHER KNOWS BEST—The Natural Way to Train Your Dog	Benj
OPEN OBEDIENCE FOR RING, HOME AND FIELD, Koehler Method of	Ko
STONE GUIDE TO DOG GROOMING FOR ALL BREEDS	S
SUCCESSFUL DOG TRAINING, The Pearsall Guide to	Pe
TEACHING DOG OBEDIENCE CLASSES—Manual for Instructors	Volhard & F
TOY DOGS, Kalstone Guide to Grooming All	Kal
TRAINING THE RETRIEVER	Ke
TRAINING TRACKING DOGS, Koehler Method of	Ko
TRAINING YOUR DOG—Step by Step Manual	Volhard & F
TRAINING YOUR DOG TO WIN OBEDIENCE TITLES	M
TRAIN YOUR OWN GUN DOG, How to	Gc
UTILITY DOG TRAINING, Koehler Method of	Ko
VETERINARY HANDBOOK, Dog Owner's Home	Carlson &

GENERAL

AMERICAN KENNEL CLUB 1884-1984—A Source Book	American Kennel
CANINE TERMINOLOGY	
COMPLETE DOG BOOK, The	Official Publicati American Kennel
DOG IN ACTION, The	
DOG BEHAVIOR, New Knowledge of	Pfaffenb
DOG JUDGE'S HANDBOOK	T
DOG PEOPLE ARE CRAZY	F
DOG PSYCHOLOGY	Wr
DOGSTEPS, The New	
DOG TRICKS	Haggerty & Ben
EYES THAT LEAD—Story of Guide Dogs for the Blind	T
FRIEND TO FRIEND—Dogs That Help Mankind	Sch
FROM RICHES TO BITCHES	Sha
HAPPY DOG/HAPPY OWNER	S
IN STITCHES OVER BITCHES	Sha
JUNIOR SHOWMANSHIP HANDBOOK	Brown & N
OUR PUPPY'S BABY BOOK (blue or pink)	
SUCCESSFUL DOG SHOWING, Forsyth Guide to	Fc
TRIM, GROOM & SHOW YOUR DOG, How to	Sau
WHY DOES YOUR DOG DO THAT?	Ber
WILD DOGS in Life and Legend	F
WORLD OF SLED DOGS, From Siberia to Sport Racing	Copp